MANIPULATION TECHNIQUES

COMMUNICATION AND PERSUASION SECRETS YOU WISH YOU KNEW

By K. Connors

© Copyright 2018 By K. Connors - All Rights Reserved.

Copyright © 2018 *Manipulation Techniques.* All rights reserved. No part of this publication may be reproduced, distributed, or transmitted in any form or by any means, including photocopying, recording, or other electronic or mechanical methods, without the prior written permission of the publisher, except in the case of brief quotations embodied in critical reviews and certain other noncommercial uses permitted by copyright law. This also includes conveying via e-mail without permission in writing from the publisher. All information within this book is of relevant content and written solely for motivation and direction. No financial guarantees. All information is considered valid and factual to the writer's knowledge. The author is not associated or affiliated with any company or brand mentioned in the book, therefore does not purposefully advertise nor receives payment for doing so.

Table of Contents

INTRODUCTION 4

CHAPTER ONE..7

EFFECTIVE COMMUNICATION STRATEGIES 7

CHAPTER TWO...15

HOW TO MANIPULATE..15

CHAPTER THREE 30

EMOTIONAL MANIPULATION AND ABUSE.............30

CHAPTER FOUR...57

PSYCHOLOGICAL MANIPULATION..........................57

CHAPTER FIVE...71

WHY ARE MANIPULATIVE TECHNIQUES IMPORTANT TO SALESPEOPLE? 71

CONCLUSION 75

INTRODUCTION

We have learned the art of manipulation since infancy. When a baby cries when their mom puts them to bed is one way of manipulation to get their way. Manipulation is at the core of every human being. With the vast knowledge that we have accumulated and ever growing technology that makes information easy to access, learning the ability to convince others is within our grasp.

Manipulating techniques nowadays come in handy thanks to the rise of the internet. Many people can look into and study the opinions and experiences of people around the world. Learning manipulating techniques can increase your overall self. Knowledge and communication skills are an important ingredient in our interactions and human relationships that can bring success to an individual. For those who are pretending to have the skill of manipulation but don't really know how to implement it, will of course, start out unsuccessful in this area. Therefore, knowing the essentials of what can make or break your strategy is an important technique.

Many techniques are used when it comes to manipulation. Even a few dirty tricks are used by people to manipulate others. In return, they also get into trouble by getting back the same karma that they intentionally practice.

There are, however, a few manipulation techniques that do not involve sly or deceiving gestures. Manipulation techniques are used mostly to outdo the techniques of others but still use the rules of fair competition. In business, we need to out-think our competitors by fulfilling the best interests of our clients and answering the needs of our customers. We can keep up with personal competition by challenging ourselves to do more and by getting the support that we need in relation to self-improvement.

We need to be aware that manipulation involves mind interaction since we can convince and persuade a person when we attempt to read his or her mind.

In the food chain, we do not act only as predators - we are also prey for others. Thus, we need to know that "not all truths are really true". People tend to believe in things even if they are just persuaded to believe that it is true.

When a salesman is selling their product, they only make you believe that it is useful. We need to understand that they are using manipulation techniques.

We also need to understand that "being perfect is an impossibility". Everybody aims to be perfect and would do anything to change their imperfections. Sometimes we can upgrade ourselves or make something better, but these changes are still not perfect in execution or result. A whitening toothepaste doesn't always give you the perfect white teeth that you want to achieve if you don't already have perfectly white teeth to begin with. Manipulation techniques only work when they are based on reality.

CHAPTER ONE

EFFECTIVE COMMUNICATION STRATEGIES

VERBAL VS. NONVERBAL COMMUNICATION

1. EFFECTIVE VERBAL COMMUNICATION

Since the beginning of the existence of human beings, even before there was an official language of any type, man has always communicated through some form of verbal communication. Although it is highly possible that communication was done through grunts and groans before the development of formal speech, the need for effective communication has always proven to be a vital necessity when it comes to advancement. While the human race has come a very long way since that tenacious beginning, one aspect has not changed; effective verbal communication is the most important tool when it comes to achieving success in any goal that requires the cooperation of more than one person.

Consider the ramifications of inadequate verbal communication; the inability to clearly express your ideas, especially if you require the help and cooperation of other people, which can lead to the failure of your proposed project, or at least the final outcome of not meeting the vision that you hold for it. Think about your own experiences, especially in school. Can you imagine what the world would be like if teachers lacked effective communication skills? A person's learning experience would be severely lacking because they wouldn't be able to understand what point the instructor is attempting to make. As a result, they would walk away from the lesson having learned nothing.

Effective verbal communication skills are also a very vital tool when it comes to achieving success in the business world. If you look at the people who occupy important positions in a company or business, you'll find that they all have one trait in common; effective verbal communication skills. While having the ability to conceive great ideas is an important attribute, without the ability to express the full vision of these ideas through verbal communication, you may as well not have had the vision to begin with.

While the art of communicating verbally is certainly not the only asset that you need for success in business and life, it certainly makes your ability to obtain success a great deal easier than without it. These skills do not apply simply to the business world. Consider what our world would be like if people did not possess the ability of effectively communicate verbally. Think about the <u>Tower of Babel</u> and you'll understand how confusing the world would be without verbal communication.

2. NON-VERBAL COMMUNICATION

This is not always a deliberate kind of communication. Unlike verbal communication, the intended message may not reach the receiver In this mode of communication. Here the participants subconsciously use gestures, signs, and pictures to convey something. Non-verbal communication plays a very important role. Perhaps sometimes more important than the verbal type in certain situations. Body language, a more common general term that is commonly used interchangeably for non-verbal communication, plays a vital part in sending strong signals about oneself.

Individuals affected with brain-related complications such as autistic spectrum disorders can lack verbal communication skills. Most of the time, these individuals lack non-verbal communication skills. They communicate with society in such a way that it appears that they do not understand the functioning and nuances of society. Such people generally do not respond talk conducted by others. They find it harder to start a conversation than others. Among non-autistic children, some children prefer to communicate through gestures and signs even though they have the ability and skill of speaking. For such children, training them to use non-verbal communication helps to improve their understanding of the world.

The most crucial period for communication abilities is said to be the first three years of life. During this period, whatever is registered in the mind stays there forever, at least on the subconscious level. For children affected by autism and related disorders, their brain is affected in such a way that their verbal communication skills are almost non-existent in some extreme cases.

Some children affected by autism spectrum disorders show extremely good skills in drawing and when using computers. In contrast, they may be poor in relation to talking and speech comprehension. Their social interactions will also tend to be more poor.

Children are supposed to make their first attempts at verbal communication when they are six months old. Later, when they are one and a half years old, they are supposed to have learned at least six words. From then onwards, their progress in vocabulary is pretty rapid. This is where children affected by diseases like autism and Asperger's syndrome are often noticed. Because of environmental or genetic problems, the brain of such children is under-developed. The majority of autism-affected children do not use non-verbal communication tools like gestures and eye contact. Some autistic children think pictorially. They can draw pictures of household objects that they are familiar with. Some teachers that specialize in the education of autistic children advocate for the use of pictures to create better awareness in autistic children about their surroundings and the environment.

The following are a few of the components of non-verbal and verbal communication that play an important role in the effectiveness of the communication process.

1. Vocal

The intonation of your speech plays an important role in non-verbal communication. A monotonic speaker has a lower impact on the target audience compared to a speaker who uses intonation properly to convey a message. Take the example of a simple word; "Yes". You can express it in many ways, exhibiting different expressions like excitement, anger, happiness, sadness, terror, mild doubt and amazement. The real difference between all of those expressions is the intonation. It is also important to note that different cultures have different meanings for the same intonation.

2. Visual

Physical appearance, facial expressions, eye movements, posture, body movements, and gestures can be considered as being effective tools to convey a message properly. We all try to interpret messages through the facial expressions and eye movements of a person.

You can easily misinterpret someone's words during your communication with him or her because you cannot see their eyes if they are covered and interpret the real meaning behind those words. Actions speak for themselves during communication. Raising of the hands, lifting the eyebrows, standing straight, direct eye contact and other such factors contribute to the effectiveness of communication. The same body movements and postures mean different things in different cultures. In one culture, nodding the head is a sign of affirmation while in another culture, moving the head right and left can mean the same thing.

3.   Tactile

Tactile movements involve the feeling of touch and are more important in one-to-one or closed group communication. Tactile communication makes use of motions like patting the back, kissing, hugging or placing an arm around the shoulder.

4.   Time

The use of timing can be viewed as an exhibition of power and a relational status defined between the speaker and the audience. A good example would be to think of the difference between the presentation of a company's CEO and a junior employee to a group of employees in a company.

5. Space

Space is used to define our territory. We classify our interaction territories with respect to our relationship with others. We feel uncomfortable if someone comes closer to us than our allowed boundary for that particular person. The comfortable interaction distance for family members is usually about 1 - 2 feet. 2 - 4 feet is considered a suitable interaction distance for friends and relatives. All business meetings and professional communications usually occur between 4 - 12 feet and public communication distance including lectures and presentations are usually considered to be over 12 feet.

CHAPTER TWO

HOW TO MANIPULATE

MIND MANIPULATION

How to manipulate is a skill that is innate to each of us. Everybody is born with it. Each individual reacts and interacts with one another. This is how manipulation works in society. It brings people in and out of our lives. It is the way that we communicate with one another.

How to manipulate is important in relation to how we communicate and relate to people. When we relate and convey our thoughts to our peers, we lure them in to listen to us and to understand our own beliefs even if they do not agree with them. We base our success on how people respond to the kind of thinking that we have. If we get favorable responses from people, we feel satisfied and that satisfaction builds up our whole being. If we somehow fail to be understood, we often resort to arguments because our subconscious fights the manipulative tactics of others. We do not want to be manipulated but somehow we tend to forget that every decision and action that we take is a product of mind manipulation by others.

The ugly truth is that we often fail to realize that we need to manipulate in order to survive and be successful. If we only aim for survival, we don't need to practice a lot of mind manipulation techniques. But should we settle for less? We want to become more than and larger than ourselves as we are in the now.

The first thing that we need to consider is that we need to understand that manipulation is not negative. Somehow, negative connotations impact the way that we deal with people. We think that being frank and direct about telling others our needs is a kind of manipulation and therefore is bad. We think that when we ask someone to do things our way, it is a kind of manipulation and so we refrain from trying to ask for help. We fail to realize that we miss the chance that could have been a new door to an opportunity.

We take pride too much in playing fair while the world is not. What we are trying to achieve, however, is not to trick everyone.

We just want to open our eyes to the opportunities that are waiting to be unlocked. If we put host a cocktail party because we want to invite others and be acquainted with somebody, who we know that can help us well with our interest and how to persuade them to help is the kind of technique that we need.

Mind manipulation is within us all. We do not need special psychic powers to be able to manipulate people and be successful. We just need to know the techniques and skillfully practice them.

MIND MANIPULATION TECHNIQUES

Mind manipulation techniques are not only prevalent on TV shows or in movies. In fact, many people today make use of mind manipulation techniques to force an individual to do something against their will. In order for you to avoid being controlled by mind manipulation techniques, you need to know the ways that a person can get into your mind and control you for personal gain or advantage.

Here are some mind manipulation techniques that you should know about to avoid being controlled by them.

1. Not all truths are really true

In most cases, people will often think that it is true if they are made to believe that it is. In fact, this method is used by sales agents to coerce other people to buy their product, even if it doesn't really benefit them that much. To be able to avoid mind manipulation techniques of this kind, don't take their words as being the undeniable truth. Spice it up with a little bit of doubt that will lead you to question the credibility and trustworthiness of their claims.

Some people have the gift of convincing people that what they are saying is the one and only thing that is true. Be alert. Do your due diligence and research their background and other people's reviews.

2. Being perfect is an impossibility

You need to realize that we are imperfect beings, and that no product and human-related actions can turn us into the perfect man or woman.

In fact, you should realize that there are certain types of mind manipulation techniques that prey on individuals who are unsure about their abilities and those who are suffering from their imperfections - or so they have been led to believe. A good example of this is television ads that say that being fair-skinned is beautiful and is the only way to be so.

3.   Illusions are considered to be nothing

One of the more common mind manipulation techniques used by scammers and fraudsters today is giving their actions a "magical" feel. Many individuals today are quite interested in the concept of magic and mysticism, and some people make use of this pandemic fascination to force an individual to perform something that will in no way produce the expected results. To protect yourself, do not be too easily bowled over by "magic." Applaud it, but don't take it as fact.

AWFUL THINGS THAT PEOPLE DO TO MANIPULATE OTHERS

In this day and age, combat is not only waged on a battlefield. Battles can also be waged inside your mind. Through psychological manipulation techniques, your enemies can actually assert sense of control over you.

However, you are not rendered completely powerless. There are different ways of countering these psychological manipulation techniques. The first step is awareness. Read about how your enemies operate so that you can better protect yourself in the future.

1. Emotional blackmailing

Emotional blackmail is one of the most commonly used manipulation techniques in this new war. How does it work exactly? A lot of people succumb to this trick because they feel as if they have no choice. Sentences like "Don't you care about the company?" or "If you really want to be my friend, you would do this for me" usually forces them to make decisions that they don't really want to.

To avoid being played with, you will have to develop a stronger sense of self. Know who you are, what your responsibilities involve, and who your real friends are. Blackmailers tend to stay away from people with strong and solid personalities.

2. Focusing on the negatives

Some people just like to put a damper on your brilliant idea by spitting out all of the things that could go wrong with it. These people are no longer offering critique. These people will usually raise questions that will raise doubts .

For example, you announce that you are thinking of flying to London for a week-long vacation. People using psychological manipulation will most likely react to your news by stating the danger of flying or the number of negative things awaiting you at the airport or on the trip itself.

These remarks are not to be taken seriously. Brush them off lightly or ignore such reactions altogether.

3. Teenage rebellion

Sadly, even those way past their teenage years like to act out as a response to your decision or whatever it is that you have just told them.

For example, you want to move out of your home to live independently. At first, everyone seems fine with it. But just as you start hunting for that perfect apartment, things start happening one after another. Some sort of personal crisis occurs in the family; your mother suddenly starts smoking again, etc. Adults who engage in teenage rebellion should know better. The easiest way to deal with this is to tell them that their efforts are futile and to go on doing what it is that you intend to accomplish.

Psychological manipulation techniques may be apparent throughout your life, but that doesn't mean that you have to give in to them. With the aforementioend points, you are now more equipped to handle different manipulative situations.

TRICKS PEOPLE USE TO MANIPULATE OTHERS

A lot of people tend to use emotional manipulation techniques to get their own way. Unfortunately, the vast majority of the population don't even realize that they are being manipulated until it is too late. Don't be lured into this trap. By learning about emotional manipulation techniques, you can protect yourself from being forced into doing things or saying things that you don't really want to.

Below are some of the sneaky tactics and dirty tricks that you have to be careful with.

1.   It's either me or him/her

Some people like to make their friends choose between them and another person. You are more pressured to choose the manipulator, for fear of losing their friendship. But a true friend would never do such a thing. This is an emotional manipulation technique that little kids use on the playground. To avoid making a decision (and one that you would probably regret either way), walk away. Let that person know that you're not going to take sides.

If they throw a huff, then that is no longer your problem. What matters is that you stayed neutral. Frankly, you'll be a lot safer that way anyway.

2.   I'll do you this favor, but don't forget that you owe me

It's really difficult to ask someone for a favor, especially when you know that they are going to exploit you right back. It is normal to ask for a favor from a friend. But there are people who will do you one favor, and they will milk you for every little thing afterwards.

When you put your foot down, they will go on a tirade about how you have no sense of gratitude and whatnot. To avoid this kind of manipulation, be careful with who you ask favors from. Remember that there is a price for everything.

3.   If you're sick, I'm dying.

We all know how this goes. Emotional manipulators will always make themselves look more like the victim than you. They crave attention, which is why they are not always happy when you get the limelight, even if it's just for a headache. There is really no getting through to a person like this.

Perhaps with the right timing, a huge and frank outburst might get through to them. However, it's easier to just let that person be and to avoid commenting.

The truth is that emotional manipulation techniques are often used by cowards. They can't do direct combat, so they will usually resort to sneaky ways to get you to do what they want. Now that you know what some of these dirty tricks, hopefully you will be able to avoid getting sucked into them.

TYPES OF MANIPULATION AND HOW TO OVERCOME THEM

Once in a while, we come across people who use manipulation to get what they want. These people can be our teachers, friends and even someone who we are in a relationship with. As much as we want to avoid these people, it's not always possible. However, there are warning signs of manipulative behavior that can tip you off.

Below are some of the signals that you have to watch out for. The warning signs of manipulative behavior are as follows:

1. Changing topics

Isn't it funny how determined some people are to change the topic when it is their behavior that is being put on the spotlight? One of the warning signs of manipulative behavior is when a person who is accused of wrongdoing shifts the conversation to something else.

Usually, the person makes himself or herself out to be the victim and speaks about the number of times that they have been maligned. What's even funnier is that the people who claim that they are not being manipulative are actually the ones who often exhibit this type of behavior.

2. Using guilt

Another one of the warning signs of manipulative behavior is when the person makes you feel guilty all the time.

It could be your boss telling you that "if you value your job, you would work overtime this week." Oh, if only people had a penny for every time their bosses told them that. The secret here is to not let guilt take over the situation. Simply tell your boss that you love your job but that you aren't able to work overtime. Don't stretch the conversation out any more than you have to.

3. Blaming it on others

When a manipulative person is once again the center of attention for something negative, they will immediately play the blame game to keep their name untarnished. With children, this can be easily corrected. In adults, this can be quite frustrating. When you find yourself trapped in such a situation, resist the urge to blame the person back. This will only cause both of you unrest and will only serve to increase the negativity of the situation. Instead, keep your cool and deal with the situation logically. If you can't do that, then it's best to walk away.

It's quite easy to spot the warning signs of manipulative behavior in other people. However, you may not always be as innocent as you think. Sometimes, manipulation begets manipulation, so don't get caught up in the process.

HOW TO MANIPULATE PEOPLE AND INFLUENCE DECISIONS

Manipulation is not always ethical if done for the wrong reasons, but in this dog eat dog world, we have to know how to manipulate people subtly and influence their decisions in an ethical manner and for the right reasons. Now, I'm not saying this so you to go out there and manipulate everyone that you meet on the street. Use these techniques for your own good and for the good of others. Most of the time, you can use these techniques to achieve positive outcomes.

With that said, we will see how to subtly influence using manipulation. While it is not possible to present a step-by-step guide as every situation is unique, there are some guidelines that you can follow to implement these ideas. Specifically, there are three things that you need to be aware of to successfully get what you want.

First of all, you should try to inject a strong emotion when trying to manipulate someone. It could be greed, fear, desire etc. If you don't do this then people will start to think critically by questioning you, and your chances of success will be remote.

Another thing that you need to know is the hot buttons of the person that you are trying to manipulate. By carefully observing the person, you will get to know what his/her hot button is

. It could be a pet, hobby or a strong feeling about a subject.

You need to be aware of social engineering techniques. Hackers use this a lot to gain access to highly secure systems. For instance, if a person in a police uniform asks you to move away from a place, will you go and examine if he is really a cop? We are conditioned to respond in a certain way to certain people. There are several other social factors that you can use for your own benefit.

Now that you know the basic guidelines, start observing people, analyze situations and try to learn from them.

CHAPTER THREE

EMOTIONAL MANIPULATION AND ABUSE

Almost everyone knows someone or a friend of someone who has been abused. Most people who are domestically abused are females, although males can certainly be abused as well. How do people become abusers? Typically, there are several factors that play into this. If a child views or witnesses either of their parents being abused or abusive while they are growing up, or if they themselves are the victims of any sort of verbal and/or physical abuse, there is a chance that they will grow up to become abusers themselves.

As a child, witnessing various forms of abuse can be traumatizing. For those who end up being the ones who endure the abuse, whether it be physical, verbal or emotional, these people tend to grow up in more sheltered environments as children. In terms of abuse, it is not uncommon for a man to beat his wife and then not have to worry about her reporting it to the police. This is because nine times out of ten, those who are abused are usually under such mental control by their abusers that it is often very difficult for them to think or see clearly about what they should do.

This can be extremely frustrating for family and friends who, from the outside, can logically see and advise the person on what to do (leave their abuser and re-start their life). However, if you've never been in an abusive situation before, then it can be difficult to empathize with someone who is going through such a time. People who are abused by their partners, spouses or other loved ones often feel ashamed and embarrassed about their situation.

Abusive relationships can also lead to the victim feeling lonely and depressed. This is dangerous because depression can act as a sort of gateway into other negative types of behavior such as drug and alcohol use or self-inflicted abuse (i.e. self mutilation-cutting themselves, etc.). It can also lead to thoughts of suicide. If you suspect that someone is being abused or that there might be something going on, you might want to consider having an intervention. An intervention is a sort of like a surprise party without the happy surprise. It is where you designate a place (usually someone's residence) and you invite friends and family who are supportive of the victim.

You also invite the person who has been abused over to confront them about the problem to let them know that they are safe and that you will help them get the help that they need. Now, this is not for everyone and needs to be deliberated over before you go forward with it. You can also take a more personal approach by simply asking the person who has been abused about what's going on. Let them know that they can speak to you in confidence. Understand that someone who has been abused will feel all sorts of emotions such as pain, frustration, anger, embarrassment, denial, and sadness. It is important to let them know that you will not judge them no matter what circumstances they have had to go through.

STYLES OF EMOTIONAL MANIPULATION

Everybody at some point in their life will have felt the icy grip of an emotional manipulator reaching inside to a part of them which they feel unable to defend no matter how hard they try.

The aim of a manipulator is to do just that, manipulate! The aim of their game is to gain control of the person who is their chosen victim. The reason for this is if they gain control of the other, then that person can be made in many ways malleable to the manipulator's desires, thereby reducing any form of threat to the manipulator. In unethical cases, it is the manipulator's paranoia and low self esteem which runs amok in their mind, giving them the impression that anybody and everybody is or could be a threat.

To overcome this and to keep themselves safe in their own mind, they will try to trick the chosen victim into feeling vulnerable, so whether or not the victim was to attack, they would usually be unable to do so

THERE ARE FOUR MAIN TYPES OF MANIPULATORS TO WATCH OUT FOR, AND THESE ARE:

1.   The Rejecter

This manipulator is a particularly nasty one and is cutting straight to the core of the deepest fear of 95% of the human race which is that of being alone. This fear is so devastating that people will do just about anything to avoid it, including trying to win the individual's affection.

2. The Insulter

This type of manipulator is "the jovial one", continually cracking the odd joke here and there, and making comments about weight gain/loss, baldness and any other area that the victim feels self-conscious about. But then when the victim says how they feel, the manipulator comes back with "I'm only kidding" or "don't get so worked up" (a hit and run attack).

3. The Intimidator

This style is more visible, but they will also try to keep it subtle. This style of manipulation works by using subtle or notable changes in the body language, heavier breathing, displaying anger, turning away, a raised voice or the appearance being ready to attack. A change made often enough using the same pattern without knowing why can often leave a victim confused and on edge, fearing the onset of physical violence.

4. The Nice Guy

This manipulator is by far one of the most devious. Posing as a friend and giving the impression that they are on the victims' side, slowly gaining their trust and willingness to open up their heart. Then, subtly dropping in degrading comments and how although the victim is a great friend, that some of their views and interests just are not right. Then the manipulator will seal the attack with 'I'm only telling you because I care', giving the victim the appearance that they are somebody to feel supported by and to turn to when in need, but in all essence, making them dependent.

Manipulators are sometimes the 'in the face' type (physical violence) but the most harmful are the emotional types who get inside their victim's mind, hijacking their emotions, leaving them confused and vulnerable and giving the manipulator all the power. If you feel uncomfortable around somebody but don't know why, chances are that you are in their grip and in many cases, both parties are totally unaware. It is your responsibility to stop the game.

HOW TO RECOGNIZE AN EMOTIONAL MANIPULATOR

Sometimes people can act in a certain way that leaves others feeling completely powerless and the victim in the game can end up confused and disorientated with no idea how it happened. This has happened to everybody at some stage in their life as people trying to 'one up on each other' is a natural process of leadership. However, in many cases, it is both sides that do not recognize what is happening. Here I will describe the "hit and run" method of emotional manipulation. This style of power control is one of the most potent as unless the victim is very strong in willpower and prepared to risk looking out of place, the odds of success stacked against you.

A hit and run method is described as the following...

Imagine one partner (Person A) has spent a long time preparing to go out for the evening and has taken put a lot of time and attention in to it but has low self-esteem. The self-esteem issue may cause the person to rely on the way that they look to feel valuable, but their inner fear is that they are not good enough. As they come downstairs to their significant other or friend, their friend may say something like "Come on, are you getting ready? It is nearly time to go out! (Implying that they do not look ready). (This is the HIT) aimed to trigger off the person's fear that, actually, they are not good enough. When person A then tries to defend themselves by replying..... "I am ready", their partner can turn back and say "Great, you look fantastic, let's go then!" (This is the RUN). If person A then asks for reassurance and says, "Well do I look OK?" the partner turns back and say "I just said you look fantastic". The insult has been placed in person A's mind and they can't really come back from it, leaving them with a feeling of inadequacy all night. This leaves their partner (person B) in complete control.

When a person feels vulnerable, they usually look to others for support and advice as they start to doubt their own value and become fearful of rejection when making errors. This is a very manipulative trick which can destroy a person's day or night, leaving some marked for years by triggering deep inner fears from the past.

The only power that a person has against this is to recognize it and genuinely ask themselves if the attacker meant to inflict injury. If they did, it may be a serious situation and be harmful for them to be around depending on if they will change or not. When working with or around a manipulator, the only power is awareness. It is very ill-advised to fight against them if they can trigger fear in you, as once you are in fear, your inner creative thoughts will evaporate and choices will become difficult. Know yourself! Know your enemy! Know your game.

HOW DO YOU KNOW WHEN YOU'RE BEING EMOTIONALLY MANIPULATED?

Most people are empathetic unless they have a personality disorder, and they understand that emotions are sacred and to be taken seriously. Most people agree that it's morally unethical to toy with someone else's emotions.

But some people - notably narcissists and psychopaths - find emotional manipulation to be a useful tactic when seeking to gain control or domination over others. Emotional manipulators have such a distorted view of their own importance in the world that they have no qualms about playing harmful mind games with other people. In extreme cases, that's just what it is - a game. The perpetrator plays the game for his or her own amusement, just to see how much he can tinker with your brain. Often these people are so skilled that you don't realize they have been hurting you until the damage is done. That's why it is important to understand these tactics to minimize the chance of someone using emotional manipulation against you.

1.   Identify emotional manipulators so you can protect yourself.

A skilled emotional manipulator can make you feel confused, unsure of your own feelings and even cause you to lose self-esteem. For example, if an emotional manipulator forgets your birthday and your feelings are hurt, they will make you feel bad when you call them out on it.

"How can you be mad at me when I've had so many other things on my mind? You know the stress I'm under, and now you're giving me even more stress." Suddenly you're babysitting someone else's angst when you are the one who was slighted.

Another classic tactic emotional manipulators will use to confuse you is when they agree with a plan and then undermine it. If, for example, they have promised to support you going back to school and say they will do more of the household chores in support of your goal, watch out. Emotional manipulators will slam the dishes around noisily while you are trying to study at the kitchen table. Or vacuum under your desk while you're sitting there. They will have great sighs or roll their eyes when you have to rush off to class. When you legitimately say that you don't feel they really want you to succeed at school, they will turn things around to make it seem like you are being unreasonable to suspect them.

Guilt is another potent tool in the emotional manipulators' toolbox. Although we are all familiar with a certain amount of guilt trips created by people who are not emotional manipulators', emotional manipulators employ this tool often and expertly. They can make you feel guilty for just about anything - sometimes even contradictory things. You talk too much, you don't talk enough. They wheedle you until you do their chores, fight their fights, and do their dirty work, often times against your will. Then they tell you that they didn't expect you to do anything. Now you feel a little crazy.

An emotional manipulator who is really good at making you doubt yourself can say one thing and later guarantee that they never said it to the point where you question your own sanity. They can turn things around, rationalize glibly and justify the most outrageous things. They can do it so expertly that you feel like your own sense of reality is altered. Maybe it is. They are so adept at lying, and without any feelings of conscience, that you wonder if you are the crazy one. When they lie about the past, they can make you question your own ability to recollect things, which can make you more dependent upon them and their memory of events. Pretty soon their version of the truth is the prevailing view.

HOW TO SPOT MANIPULATION

We all want to get our needs met, but unethical manipulators use underhanded methods. This type of manipulation is a way to covertly influence someone with indirect, deceptive, or abusive tactics. Manipulation may seem benign, friendly or even flattering as if the person has your highest concerns in mind, and in some cases it is. But in reality, it may be to achieve an ulterior motive. Other times, it is veiled as hostility and when abusive methods are used, the objective is merely power. You may not realize that you're being unconsciously intimidated.

If you grew up being manipulated, it's harder to discern what's going on because it feels familiar. You might have a gut feeling of discomfort or anger, but on the surface, the manipulator may use words that are pleasant, ingratiating, reasonable, or that play on your guilt or sympathy, so then you override your instincts and don't know what to say. Co-dependents have trouble being direct and assertive, and may use manipulation to get their own way. They are also easy prey for being manipulated by narcissists, borderline personalities, sociopaths, and other co-dependents, including addicts.

MANIPULATIVE TACTICS

Favorite weapons of these types of manipulators are guilt, complaining, comparing, lying, denying (including excuses and rationalizations), feigning ignorance, or innocence (the "Who me!?" defense), blame, bribery, undermining, mind games, assumptions, "foot-in-the-door," reversals, emotional blackmail, evasiveness, forgetting, fake concern, sympathy, apologies, flattery, and gifts and favors. Manipulators often use guilt by saying it directly or by implication, "After all I've done or you," or chronically behaving needy and helpless. They may compare you negatively to someone else or rally imaginary allies to their cause, saying that, "Everyone", "Even so and so thinks XYZ," or "Everyone says xyz about you."

Some individuals will deny promises, agreements, or conversations, or start an argument and blame you for something that you didn't do to get sympathy and power.

This approach can be used to break a date, promise, or agreement. Parents routinely manipulate with bribery - everything from "Finish your dinner to get dessert," to "No video games until your homework is done." A close friend of mine was bribed with a promise of a car, which he needed in order to commute to summer school on the condition that he agreed to go to the college that his parents had chosen rather than the one he had decided on. He always regretted taking the bribe. When you do, it undermines your self-respect.

Manipulators often voice assumptions about your intentions or beliefs and then react to them as if they were true in order to justify their feelings or actions, all the while denying what you say in the conversation. They may act as if something has been agreed upon or decided when it hasn't been in order to ignore any input or objection that you might have.

The "foot-in-the-door" technique is making a small request that you agree to, which is followed by the real request. It's harder to say no because you've already said yes. The reversal turns your words around to mean something you didn't intend. When you object, manipulators turn the tables on you so that they're the injured party. Now it's about them and their complaints, and you're on the defensive. The fake concern is sometimes used to undermine your decisions and confidence in the form of warnings or worry about you.

EMOTIONAL BLACKMAIL

Emotional blackmail is abusive manipulation that may include the use of rage, intimidation, threats, shame, or guilt. Shaming you is a method to create self-doubt and make you feel insecure. It can even be couched in a compliment: "I'm surprised that you of all people... you'd stoop to that!" A classic ploy is to frighten you with threats, anger, accusations, or dire warnings, such as "At your age, you'll never meet anyone else if you leave," or "The grass isn't any greener," or playing the victim: "I'll die without you."

Blackmailers may also frighten you with anger, so you sacrifice your needs and wants. If that doesn't work, they sometimes suddenly switch to a lighter mood. At this point you may be so relieved that you are willing to agree to whatever is asked.

They might bring up something that you feel guilty or ashamed about from the past as leverage to threaten or shame you, such as "I'll tell the children ABC if you do XYZ."

Victims of blackmailers who have certain personality disorders, such as borderline or narcissistic PD, are prone to experiencing a psychological FOG, which stands for Fear, Obligation, and Guilt, an acronym created by Susan Forward. The victim is made to feel afraid to cross the manipulator, feels obligated to comply with his or her requests and feels too guilty not to do so. Shame and guilt can be used directly with put-downs or accusations that you're "selfish" (the worse vice to many co-dependents) or that "You only think of yourself," "You don't care about me," or that "You have it so easy."

CO-DEPENDENCY

Co-dependents are rarely assertive. They may say whatever they think someone wants to hear to get along or be loved, but then later they do what they want. This is also known as passive-aggressive behavior. Rather than answer a question that might lead to a confrontation, they're evasive, change the topic, or use blame and denial (including excuses and rationalizations) to avoid being wrong. Because they find it so hard to say no, they may say yes, followed by complaints about how difficult accommodating the request will be. When confronted, because of their deep shame, co-dependents have difficulty accepting responsibility, so they deny responsibility and blame or make excuses and empty apologies to keep the peace.

They use charm and flattery and offer favors, help, and gifts in order to be accepted and loved. Criticism, guilt, and self-pity are also used to manipulate others to get what they want: "Why do you only think of yourself and never ask or help me with my problems? I helped you." Acting like a victim is a way to manipulate with guilt. Addicts routinely deny, lie, and manipulate to protect their addiction. Their partners also manipulate. For example, by hiding or diluting an addict's drugs or alcohol or through other covert behavior. They may also lie or tell half-truths to avoid confrontations or to control the addict's behavior.

PASSIVE-AGGRESSION

Passive-aggressive behavior can also be used to manipulate. When you have trouble saying no, you might agree to things that you don't want to, and then get your way by forgetting, being late, or doing it half-heartedly. Typically, passive-aggression is a way of expressing hostility. Forgetting "on purpose" conveniently avoids what you don't want to do and gets back at your partner - like forgetting to pick up your spouse's clothes from the cleaners. Sometimes this is done unconsciously, but it is still a way of expressing anger. More hostile is offering desserts to your dieting partner, as one example.

HOW TO HANDLE MANIPULATORS

The first step is to know who you are dealing with. They know your triggers! Study their tactics and learn their favorite weapons. Build your self-esteem and self-respect. This is your best defense! Learn to be assertive and set boundaries.

HOW TO DEAL WITH EMOTIONAL MANIPULATORS?

It's important that you know how to deal with emotional manipulators. I think there are only a few areas where it is more rife than in conventional health care. You will be unlikely to find it in holistic health care, perhaps not impossible, but this is unlikely because the whole area is much more relaxed.

You have probably witnessed this yourself at some stage. Doctors, veterinarians, and their staff feel that only they have the answers to proper health care and so tend to use any way available that is guaranteed to arouse guilt in you. This way you are far more likely to agree to their methods.

Guilt is the main response that you will feel when you are being emotionally blackmailed. This may develop into worry and a stream of 'what ifs'. Both guilt and worry are disempowering emotions that have nothing to do with truth, or with proper health care.

If you choose not to vaccinate your child or your pet, you are likely to face emotional blackmail if you need to consult a doctor, hospital or vet on any other, totally unrelated, matter.

If you have not taken the medication suggested which is claimed to prevent or treat disease and a blood test *suggests* (I use that word deliberately as no test is totally conclusive) that the discase is present, you will probably face a barrage of emotional abuse; sometimes this is watered down but not always. If you choose not to go down the path of conventional cancer treatment, you are likely to be pressurized and sometimes even harassed.

Emotional manipulators come from a very weak position. If something is good, there is no need to use any tactics. It is curious, that in conventional medicine which is so widely used, there is still a need to use such tactics. Are they afraid of something? Perhaps you will discover that it isn't all that it is cracked up to be?

Once guilt and worry have been aroused in you, you are in a weak position. You can never make a sound judgment. You cannot feel what is right for you, your child or your pet. Those voices have been drowned out. It's almost too late to make an informed choice. But not quite.

You need to learn how to deal with emotional blackmail before it arises again. And the first thing to do is to recognize that it is happening. To acknowledge that guilt and worry has been intentionally instilled in you. It is unlikely that you will get rid of it that quickly, so you need to work with it. Once you have acknowledged within yourself that this is happening, become conscious of your breathing. Keep it deep and slow. Don't let it quicken. Quick breathing speeds up your heart, and then all is lost.

Listen politely to the person. Don't let their possible lack of manners or respect upset you in anyway. Don't agree with anything they say, simply thank them for their concern and say that you will think about it. Smile slightly if you feel that helps. Then extract yourself (and your child or pet) as quickly as possible.

It is possible they have a valid concern, but you will only see that when you can be calm and objective. Don't throw the baby out with the bath water. Make sure you are calm, objective and ARE looking at all the possibilities you know about before taking any action.

You may like to get a second opinion or do some research yourself. You may be coming from a completely different mindset. Perhaps a more healthy one.

One thing is certain though; when you are made to feel guilty or worried because of your actions, you are not being treated with respect. Maybe it is time to find someone who will.

Learning how to deal with emotional manipulators is very empowering because it firmly puts you in the driver's seat. None of us have all of the answers, or anywhere near so. We all are best guided by our experiences, our feelings, and yes, our intuition. Yes, you may make mistakes and you may feel regret. But this will be because you cared enough to try to make the right choices, not because you were over-ruled or manipulated.

WAYS TO PROTECT YOURSELF FROM EMOTIONAL MANIPULATORS

The devastation that emotional predators can cause in your life is insidious and serious. These people can wear you down until you are a depressed, defeated shadow of the person that you once were. That's why it's important to recognize the tactics they will use to dominate you and set strict boundaries to protect yourself from them.

Remember, you cannot change the emotional manipulator. But you can change the way that you respond to them. Once you identify the tactics they are using, you can be prepared to change your behavior to protect yourself from their abuse.

1. Stand up for yourself: When an emotional manipulator puts you down and makes you feel confused or helpless, fight back. Don't let them get away with it. Here's an example of an emotional manipulator trying to make you feel bad. The

emotional manipulator is doing a task, say, cleaning up the cat litter. Here's the conversation:

You: Let me help you with that.

Emotional Manipulator: No, I've got it.

You: Okay.

Emotional Manipulator: (cleaning cat box) Sigh.

You don't say a word. You offered; the emotional manipulator refused your help. Now the emotional manipulator is heaving great sighs and making sounds of distress, as you knew they would do. They finally finish the job.

Emotional Manipulator: It would have been nice to have had some help.

You: I offered, but you refused.

Emotional Manipulator: You don't know how to clean a cat box properly.

You: Of course I do. You know that as well as I do.

The key is to stand up for yourself and refuse to accept the emotional manipulator's gambit. Once an emotional manipulator finds a tactic that works with you, you're sunk. They'll use it against you again and again.

2. Set clear boundaries: This is sometimes difficult since an emotional manipulator can be so devious that you don't even comprehend all their maneuvers. Begin by having a conversation with the emotional manipulator about what you will absolutely not accept anymore. Acknowledge that you have put up with the emotional manipulator's behavior in the past, but you will no longer enable the abuse. Tell them that you expect them to stop name-calling, using sarcasm to put you down, raising their voice to yell at you, cursing, attacking your character or any other behavior that you find disconcerting.

3. Establish firm consequences: When an emotional manipulator violates the boundaries that you have set - and they surely will - they should know that there will be consequences. Tell them you will no longer engage with them. You will leave the room. Then do it. Go somewhere else and listen to music. Take a bath. Wear headphones so you can't hear them. Do whatever YOU want to do. Whatever it takes. Be prepared to do this over and over until they change their behavior, or leave. You will have

to stand your ground and not give in, ever. Do not bluff. Establish only the consequences that you are prepared to carry out.

4. Trust your instinct: When an emotional manipulator attempts to get you to do their dirty work, especially if it makes you feel uncomfortable, listen to yourself.

If you don't want to do it, even though they seem helpless to do it themselves, refuse politely. You may even say something like, "I have every confidence you can work this out yourself." Make decisions that feel right to you, not the emotional manipulator. Many emotional manipulator's have the ability to suck the energy from a room and from you. Resist that. Seek out positive emotions and what feels good.

5. Know when to call it quits: Sometimes relationships and friendships just can't be saved. These manipulators are emotionally weak and need to torment and control in order to feel emotionally secure and fulfilled. Individuals like this definitely need help, but they seldom recognize this fact. If you're in a relationship with an emotional

manipulator, you can attempt to get them help, but don't be surprised if they refuse.

CHAPTER FOUR

PSYCHOLOGICAL MANIPULATION

The art of subtly manipulating someone psychologically is one that can get you a long way in life, help you to be a great leader and assist you in getting your own way. It might seem like it's not particularly moral, and that is because it probably isn't, but whether it is or not really depends on how you use it.

There are many secrets to being successful in psychological warfare and subtly affecting someone's beliefs or opinions. One is to quickly identify the aspects of a person so that you can better understand them. This is often known as the 'art of deduction' or the 'science of deduction' as taught by Sherlock Holmes. In NLP (Neuro-Linguistic Programming), a person is taught to quickly deduce what kind of 'processing' a person uses so as to be able to appeal to their sensibilities. If someone says 'see here', then perhaps they process information 'visually' and appealing to that sense will have the most impact on them, whereas if they say 'listen to me', you should maybe attempt a more auditory assault.

As well as using the art of deduction and NLP to identify the nature of a person, you can also use some tried and tested methods to appeal to a broad range of people. One is to develop 'rapport' by gently mirroring someone's gestures and movements. Another is to appeal to facts and statistics or to involve emotion in your approach to try and get someone to agree with your point of view.

PSYCHOLOGICAL MANIPULATION TECHNIQUES

You've probably heard about manipulative psychology, how you can use it or even how it's almost certainly being used on you to get you to do things that other people want you to do. Either way, it's useful to know some of the psychological manipulation techniques that exist so that you can either build up your defense mechanisms or covertly use them on other people (for their overall good, of course).

1.   Putting down the other person

Normally if you put someone else down verbally, it runs a very high risk of coming across as a personal attack. This raises their defenses and won't show you in a very good light - not much good if you're trying to get them to do something you want.

But humor lowers the barriers. After all, with the exception of some alternative comedians, jokes are funny and not normally nasty. If you can turn your potential put-down into a joke, it will still work the same way but it won't leave the visible scars.

One easy way of doing this is to put the joke into the third person: "Other people..." that kind of thing. Then if the other person still guesses that it's really aimed at them, qualify it with a throwaway line such as "present company excepted, of course".

2.   Use made-up truths

The internet does this all the time. So do adverts. Those 8 out of 10 cats whose owners preferred a particular brand were a carefully selected bunch of felines. By limiting the sample size and carefully phrasing the question in a way that even a politician would be envious, they got the answer that they set out to get.

Most people won't question statements of "fact" especially if you use them sparingly and qualify them with something like "a survey I read about said..."

It's even better if you cast doubt on the fact. This is because the seeds have been planted in the other person's mind. A bit like the moon landings where a good-sized portion of the world questions whether they ever happened. Whether they did or not - personally I think that a spacecraft landed as shown but I'm less sure about who was in it or whether they survived the radiation and other nasties - the seeds of doubt have been planted. If it was so easy back at the end of the 1960's, why, with all our technology improvements, hasn't anyone gone back? Not even the Russians or the Chinese for some one-upmanship. I digress.

OK, so the moon landings don't affect most of us much of the time. We can use other so-called truths to help persuade other people round to our way of thinking and manipulate their thoughts surprisingly easily.

3.   Create an illusion

You don't have to be David Copperfield or Criss Angel to do this. They spend weeks and months practicing their "impossible" tricks. Instead, you can build up a lot of supporting evidence to help you prove whatever it is you're trying to manipulate.

Street scammers use stooges and patsys. That takes quite a bit of work and requires the help of other people. Planting the seeds of ideas in other people's minds works brilliantly for illusions. Give them a few days or weeks and they do almost all of the manipulation themselves. Then they come up with their own brilliant idea that is actually what you wanted in the first place. Result.

HOW TO PROTECT YOURSELF FROM PSYCHOLOGICAL MANIPULATION?

If you think that psychological manipulation only happens in movies and interrogation rooms, think again. It's something that can easily infiltrate your everyday life. You might experience it in work, school or even while you're out buying groceries at the supermarket.

Granted, being manipulated to buy chicken instead of beef might not sound like such a big deal, but what about bullying in school or at work? Psychological manipulation tactics often get worse as time goes by.

Unless you take action and protect yourself, these situations might eventually lead to harmful effects on your mental, emotional and physical health.

1. Be aware

Francis Bacon said that knowledge is power. And he's definitely right about this one. By arming yourself with information or by just being aware of psychological manipulation, you are already protecting yourself.

How can you solve a problem if you don't even know there is one to begin with? Honestly, just being where you are right now and reading this book already sends you three or four steps ahead of your problem.

2. Stick to your guns

This really isn't the easiest thing in the world to do. Sometimes, you just can't help but be swayed by other people. However, know that once you resist the urge to follow someone else's lead, it will all be worth it.

You will get the feeling of overcoming something huge and you'll even see yourself in a new light, which in turn, will only serve to empower you more. This isn't the same as being highly stubborn, mind you.

3. Build yourself up

Targets of psychological manipulation are oftentimes those who do not really have a lot of confidence in themselves. If you're insecure, other people will just try to use your lack of self-confidence to control you.

For example, if you're someone who cares a lot about your appearance, another person can easily say something to trigger a reaction from you.

In order to prevent yourself from being victimized by such tactics, make sure you're comfortable with who you are. Look for all your good points instead of dwelling on your not-so-good characteristics. Be grateful for all of the great things happening in your life.

Don't let psychological manipulation get to you. Moving to a new school or leaving your job isn't always the solution to your problem. Running away won't help you get anywhere. All you get is a change of environment but not a change of mindset. Just remember to be alert, on your toes, be firm with your decisions and believe in yourself.

PSYCHOLOGICAL MANIPULATION WITH SUBLIMINAL TECHNOLOGY

Don't worry, the subject of the matter here is primarily yourself and this isn't about manipulation per se - but instead, it is about re-programming your mind and re-positioning it so that it brings about success for you in all you do by letting you take back control of life from a subconscious mind that is irate, negative and honed by a lifetime of bad experiences. This is subliminal technology - technology that gives you the tools to mold your mind to the shape you want it to be in. We call it psychological manipulation with subliminal technology' but we should actually name it regaining the power of your mind - because this is exactly what this part is talking about.

I'll concentrate on the aspects of technology like flash messages and subliminal sounds engineered with low-level messages and sounds designed to reprogram the mind. What they do in fact is either break down the wall of conscious thinking or just bypass it and get right to the core that matters - the subconscious.

In summary, the conscious mind is the one that we are "aware" of - the still, small voice in our head comes from it is the sponge that absorbs messages from the world, direct or indirect and uses it to build your character, your attitude and your state of mind. While it does go deeper than that, that is the basic gist of the idea. The subconscious takes instructions directly from the conscious mind and it is the machinery that drives the human spirit and soul.

We get lazy because of our subconscious. We stay constant in our ways because of our subconscious. Our character defects and bad habits are all due to the subconscious mind perpetuating it as a routine that we sometimes do not feel or just deny completely. So what happens? Well, we need to reprogram our mind, cleaning off the dirt and mental grime that has clogged it up. The brush and the broom would be the subliminal technologies that can get straight to the heart of the matter.

Inserting the messages directly means that we are trumping the conscious mind and putting in the instructions that we want to straight into the subconscious mind. Instantly, they begin to get recruited into the neural matrix and reproduced within the cortex and cerebrum of our mind, piggybacking on the electrical impulses and delivered to every part of our body.

This excellent delivery system means that the messages that tell us to stop smoking, tell us that eating too much is bad, tell us that we have to be happy and positive get wired into our nature and wired into our everyday lives.

This is the positive kind of psychological manipulation that subliminal technology can bring about. Somewhere in there is the latent potential to be smarter, tougher, more ambitious and more driven in life – even healthier and happier, and it can be unlocked with the use of subliminal technology, a technology that is easily available on the internet.

USING MANIPULATIVE PSYCHOLOGY FOR SELF IMPROVEMENT

Manipulative psychology is a powerful tool to reprogram your mind to achieve success in everything that you do and to deal with people who try to manipulate you by identifying their secret maneuvers. Learning this technique is not difficult; it comes naturally to successful and influential people.

Manipulative psychology is a step by step process that teaches you to be vibrant, confident and a dominant player in your profession as well as your non-professional relationships. It's a scientific procedure that hones your social interactive skills to make you a natural leader in your social circle.

It's a sure fire way to make you extremely popular and the most admired person in your group. You will learn to become extroverted and an expert at handling difficult people. You can use these ideas to charm anyone into having a positive response to you.

You can use these techniques to rewire your thinking process and change your actions and behavior accordingly. Success eludes most people because they are too shy or hesitant to undertake a new project or idea, so the primary step to change yourself is by controlling your thoughts. Your thoughts are the blueprints to your success in the outer world. You must, therefore, get rid of all negative thoughts that constantly hinder your growth as an individual by draining all of your creative energy. One of the best ways of doing that is by first identifying all negative emotions and thoughts, and then detaching yourself from them.

Learn to ignore them and they'll disappear by themselves. In order to do that you must engage yourself in some meaningful activity of your interest. Another way of getting rid of negative thoughts is by replacing them with positive affirmations such as "I can" instead of "I can't".

One of the most powerful techniques of self-improvement through Manipulative Psychology is the process of Visualization. You must actually visualize yourself possessing all of the positive traits that you wish to acquire. Your subconscious mind is endowed with the power to turn your thoughts into actions. This is an effective way of manipulating your sub-conscious mind into turning your dreams into reality.

You can use these techniques on others to get them to do anything you want them to. For instance, you can use the power of visualization to make your clients visualize that the project you are proposing is of immense importance and vital for their growth. If you are an employer, then you can use this technique to make your employees feel important to their organization and hence, you can motivate them to reach their maximum productivity.

If you are an employee then you can persuade your boss into giving you a reasonable salary hike or promotion by using the persuasive skills that you can learn through manipulative psychology.

Manipulative psychology uses the art of interpreting body language to make your personality more appealing to others. You can also use this knowledge to accurately detect your client's current mindset and to interpret their emotions such as irritation, boredom, anger, confidence etc and then go on to successfully persuade them to give you a positive response when they are in their most responsive mindset. Manipulative psychology can give you a cutting edge over your competitors, boost your sales, and give you the success that you truly deserve.

CHAPTER FIVE

WHY ARE MANIPULATIVE TECHNIQUES IMPORTANT TO SALESPEOPLE?

We have all been inspired by the pioneers of sales of the past years that we now know as sales gurus. By the means of traditional sales techniques, they have achieved greatness, and these techniques have been our references. The reality is that manipulative tactics draw their source from traditional sales techniques.

First, it is imperative to know what the emotional manipulative techniques are. Second, by being aware of them, it is also important to avoid them because it is a crime to use manipulative techniques to win over prospects.

TRADITIONAL VS. MODERN SALES APPROACHES

A lot of has changed in buying customer behavior due to globalization, such as the customer attaching value to the relationship. Potential customers want to purchase solutions for current and future use, and then manipulator salespeople act as if they have ignored the modern principle. So, the worry of selling alone ties salespeople to both traditional and modern closing techniques. The confusing part here is whether to use the two selling approaches or to choose one over the other. Not every traditional sales tactic is perfect, so the key part is the self-willingness to differentiate what are the necessary prerequisites.

The sales adventure playground is actually mixed with a variety of prospective customers with various needs. The reality is that each will respond differently, but it's up to the salesperson's wishes to decide what to do in terms of selling. By using manipulative strategy to sell, we have to bear in mind that eventually one way or another, the truth will be out. Remember that the main goal is not about simply selling, but to generate repeat purchases from the same customer.

Manipulation

Manipulation, according to various definitions, is the act of playing with someone's emotions with the purpose of attaining self-interested goals. Is it really necessary to manipulate prospects' minds by telling them statements like "Today is the last day of sales"? Is that really the only way to close a deal? However, playing with a potential customer's mind to create fear in them using such approaches has now become obsolete. Clients have shifted their method of creating value, while it is also time for salespeople to adopt strategies to the present philosophy.

How do we communicate and avoid manipulation during sales?

Persuasion

Persuasion is allowed in sales, but what matters is the motive behind it. Asking qualifying questions should not be abused, but instead, it should be maximized to understand whether we fit in to bring solutions to clients. Ethical practices in sales are internally driven, not externally motivated. If you think that your solution will help your client lower his/her company profit margin, why would you then enforce manipulation?

Therefore, a sales practice based upon manipulation is a dangerous weapon against one's own product, solution or company. Any slight mistake, and the damage will be huge and difficult to catch up with. Intentions with the purpose of convincing prospects to achieve self-benefits should be avoided by all means. Thus, even sales techniques should conform to current sales practices.

CONCLUSION

Both persuasion and manipulation are methods of convincing people to do something, to get them to react favorably to your ideas or to change their thinking to match yours. They are based on principles of human action and interaction. Although the two are similar to some extent, they follow different styles and their results are usually different.

A salesperson's job is to persuade people. However, the careless adoption of persuasion techniques may lead to manipulation. Salespeople should understand the two concepts and try to avoid using manipulation to make sales. Here are some of the differences between them.

Persuasion is ethical while manipulation is not. Persuasion is about influencing people to go with something that they need. On the other hand, manipulation is about convincing people to go with something that you want. Well-executed persuasion will build loyalty and trust in your customers resulting in repeat purchases. Although manipulation can build trust and loyalty as well, it will only be in the short-term and will be followed by permanent detachment. Forceful persuasion is manipulation and you should avoid it.

The aim of manipulation is to control. Using manipulation will result in win and loss situations. Sometimes you will make sales and other times your targets will outsmart you and fail to make any purchases. In contrast to manipulation, persuasion aims at boosting the self-esteem of the target customers. It involves treating them well and showing them respect. This will result in the target customers reacting positively to your offers.

When trying to make a sale, you should ask questions to understand your customer's situation. You need to be open and present the facts of your products in a positive light and show how they will benefit the users. This is what persuasion is all about. Manipulation, on the other hand, involves playing with the emotions of other parties and leaving out useful information. Manipulators normally imply and make up non-existent facts.

Manipulation is self-centered. A manipulator only does what he or she feels is beneficial to themself and doesn't care who gets hurt in the process. This is a bad business practice which will end up with you losing your clients.

Persuasion aims to serve. A persuader knows the importance of his or her customers and aims to take their interests to heart. A persuader builds strong and long-lasting relationships with their customers.

While both manipulators and persuaders understand the importance of motivation in influencing decision-making, manipulators use this knowledge to their advantage while persuaders use it to the advantage of their customers. An understanding of these concepts is very important for every salesperson. Remember, a salesperson doesn't only sell products, but they market themselves as well.

Effective persuasion techniques will result in favorable responses from your targets. However, although manipulation may help you get further, it is usually damaging in the long-run and you should avoid it at all costs. An understanding of persuasion techniques will not only increase your success in life, but it will also help to grow strong bonds with others, thus, winning their trust and loyalty.